A Goal

with a

A Goal Is a Dream with a Deadline

*Extraordinary Wisdom
for Entrepreneurs, Managers,
& Other Smart People*

LEO B. HELZEL & FRIENDS

McGraw-Hill, Inc.

New York   San Francisco   Washington, D.C.   Auckland   Bogotá
Caracas   Lisbon   London   Madrid   Mexico City   Milan
Montreal   New Delhi   San Juan   Singapore
Sydney   Tokyo   Toronto

Library of Congress Cataloging-in-Publication Data
Helzel, Leo B.
    A goal is a dream with a deadline : extraordinary wisdom for
entrepreneurs, managers, and other smart people / Leo B. Helzel and friends.
        p.   cm.
    Includes index.
    ISBN 0-07-028262-5
    1. Entrepreneurship—Quotations, maxims, etc.   2. Industrial
management—Quotations, maxims, etc.   3. Business—Quotations,
maxims, etc.   4. Success in business—Quotations, maxims, etc.
I. Title.
HB615.H345   1995
658.4'21—dc20   95-19908
                                                                    CIP

1 2 3 4 5 6 7 8 9 0 DOC / DOC 9 0 9 8 7 6 5

ISBN 0-07-028262-5

*The sponsoring editor for this book was David Conti, the editing supervisor was Fred Dahl,
and the production supervisor was Suzanne Rapcavage. It was set in Palatino by Inkwell
Publishing Services.*

Printed and bound by R. R. Donnelley & Sons Company.

To my wife, Florence,
who gave me the idea for this book
and encouraged me to write it.

Contents

Foreword

*"It is not enough to dream;
one must know how to dream."*

Charles Baudelaire

In the time it takes you to read this sentence, some company, somewhere in the world, will improve its technology, introduce a novel product or service, or enter a new market. The pace is staggering and inexorable. How can most businesses, particularly new ventures, succeed with this brutal competition?

Entrepreneurship–not doing business as usual–can be the answer. This is the age of the entrepreneur, a risk taker who perceives a unique opportunity and creates a can-do, customer-responsive organization to pursue it. Thousands of successful entrepreneurs–Bill Gates of Microsoft, Ted Turner of CNN, and Fred Smith of FedEx, to name a few–have amassed fortunes for their investors and themselves in building companies that operate under new guidelines. This is the first book to describe the entrepreneurial process through a series of pragmatic and sometimes humorous one-liners. The quips span the evolution of a company from the birth of an idea to emergence of an organization, through profitable implementation and international expansion, to going public and beyond.

These guidelines are mostly imperatives, more positive than negative, that entrepreneurs use in operating their businesses and in philosophizing about them. You may recognize some of these maxims because one-liners are a form of folk wisdom. Over the past 25 years, I've used many of them as tools for my entrepreneurship classes at the University of California at Berkeley.

More than eighty successful entrepreneurs, executives, professionals, business academics, and I contributed maxims on entrepreneurship. Chief executive officers (CEOs) expounded on decision making and management; top-notch sales people outlined the essence of marketing and sales strategy; financiers revealed insights into attracting capital; attorneys spoke to client relations; accountants instructed on crunching the numbers. Sophisticated business solutions are presented in guidelines that are easy to understand and remember.

The "entrepreneurial spirit" symbolizes change, creating the new–ideas, technology, systems, products, companies–cutting red tape and bureaucracy. It pertains to almost any person, activity and organization, including governments. Everyone is getting into the act. Accordingly, these guidelines apply equally to CEOs and employees of all organizations, from fledgling ventures to the largest companies— even non-profits.

Established businesses face enormous pressures to improve profits, reduce costs, downsize, and minimize layers of supervision. Many managements have responded by decentralizing and splitting their companies into several autonomous operations that respond quickly to customers' present *and* future needs. The entrepreneurial executives who are chosen to head these newly-formed units are often known as "intrapreneurs"–entrepreneurs within established organizations.

In today's fast-paced world, entrepreneurs, intrapreneurs, and other leaders must tirelessly innovate, take large risks and persevere. Having technological advantage or being first in a market never guarantees long-term financial security. Successful business people and their employees know that their security lies in the profitable operation of their companies and that they must constantly strive to build and rebuild their businesses to stay in the race. They recognize the truths inherent in these guidelines and the Ten Commandments of Entrepreneurship that follow.

Leo B. Helzel
Haas School of Business
University of California, Berkeley

The Ten Commandments of Entrepreneurship

*Accomplish them with enthusiasm
and everyone in the venture
will make money and
have fun doing it.*

I.   Set your goal and go for it.

II.   Be tireless and persevere.

III.   Focus on niche markets.

IV.   Be decisive and implement decisions quickly.

V.   Listen and be responsive to customers,
suppliers, employees, and investors.

VI.   Maintain CFN–Cash Flow Now.

VII.   Innovate.

VIII. Minimize layers of management.

IX.   Maximize profits by keeping costs low and productivity high.

X.   Believe in yourself.

Acknowledgments

This book is more of a collaboration than most. I have been fortunate to have partners in this effort who have made an extraordinary commitment to the book. Among them, in alphabetical order:

James H. Clark, director of the University of California Press, who offered encouragement and savvy advice on getting the book published.

David J. Conti and Laura B. Friedman, respectively editorial director and senior marketing director, Business McGraw-Hill, who believed in the book and made it happen with enthusiasm and style.

William A. Hasler, dean of the Haas School of Business, who saw the potential for this kind of book and supported the effort among faculty and business leaders.

Richard H. Holton, Ph.D., professor emeritus and former dean of the Haas School, who initiated the school's entrepreneurship program with me in 1970. His expertise in reviewing many drafts of the book has been a major factor in completing the task.

Acknowledgments

David Irons, Haas public affairs director, who has been my chief collaborator in this endeavor. Much of the style of presentation came from David.

James Karr, a former business associate, who did early research for the book.

Deborah L. Kirshman, fine arts editor of the University of California Press and my daughter, who reviewed the book to ensure that the average reader would easily understand and enjoy it.

Richard A. Moran, Ph.D., partner of Price Waterhouse and author of *Never Confuse a Memo with Reality* and other books, who encouraged me to use one-liners to cover the entrepreneurial process.

Luther A. Nichols, retired editor of Doubleday, who offered valuable suggestions on the format and tips on doing business with editors and publishers.

Matt Richtel, a business writer for the *Oakland Tribune,* who helped me focus the early drafts and stimulated me to think of the book in new ways.

Herbert E. Stansbury, cartoonist, author, business executive, and board chairman emeritus of San Francisco Federal Savings, who drew his cartoons especially for this book.

Kathleen Wall, my assistant, who is my right arm in everything I attempt to do.

Robert Zembsch, a business associate, former student, and long-term friend, who has selflessly devoted himself to creating and editing one-liners and helping me organize the book.

Contributors

I've been using one-liners in teaching for more than fifty years. Sometimes, I don't have a clue where they come from. Most often they are neither planned nor rehearsed. The best of them are a form of folk wisdom that has become part of language used in business.

During my professional, business, and teaching years, I have made many friends who are as fascinated with the entrepreneurial process as I am. When I told them of the idea for this book, more than eighty responded with one-liners from their own experience. I have selected the best of these entries (in my opinion), edited them for style of presentation and added them to my own zingers to make up this book.

Their contributions to *A Goal Is a Dream with a Deadline* were also inspired by the thought that the book would popularize the entrepreneurial process, inspire more teaching of it, and benefit the programs on entrepreneurship at the Haas School of Business, University of California, Berkeley. All my net royalties have been donated to the Haas School.

CONTRIBUTORS

I am grateful to all of the following contributors for their time, ideas, entries and generosity:

Victor D. Alhadeff, Chairman and CEO, Catapult, Inc.

Sheldon Appel, President and CEO, Shoe Carton Corporation

Richard S. Atlas, Limited Partner, Goldman, Sachs & Co.

Leonard B. Auerbach, Ph.D., President and CEO, Tuttle & Auerbach Securities, Inc.

David Babbel, Ph.D., Professor, The Wharton School, University of Pennsylvania

Elizabeth T. Ball, Executive Secretary to the General Manager, San Francisco Symphony

Saul Belilove, Founder and Retired President of the Belilove Company

William H. Bentley, Partner (retired), Arthur Andersen and Co.

Adam Berman, President, Education Partners and Lecturer in Entrepreneurship, Haas School

Donald B. Bibeault, President, Bibeault & Associates, Inc.

Thomas H. Byers, Consulting Professor, Stanford University

Earl F. Cheit, Ph.D., Chairman, Shaklee Corporation, Professor and Dean Emeritus, Haas School

Michael N. Chetkovich, Senior Advisor, Haas School and former Chairman of Deloitte and Touche (Haskins & Sells)

F. Leighs Church, President and CEO, Key Group Technology, Inc.

Howard Cohen, President and CEO, Micro Computer Support, Inc.

Michael Cookson, President and CEO, SportsLab, Inc.

William F. Cronk, President, Dreyer's Grand Ice Cream

John S. Cullison, Vice President, Bank of America

John L. de Benedetti, President, Cypress Properties

Terri Dial, Executive Vice President, Wells Fargo Bank

Giuseppe F. Dose, Vice President, Bank of America

Alvin Duskin, Chairman and CEO, Trinity Flywheel Batteries, Inc.

Alvin M. Eicoff, Founder, A. Eicoff and Co.

Jerome S. Engel, Executive Director, Lester Center for Entrepreneurship and Innovation, Haas School

George W. Ettelson, Private Investor

Donald S. Farnsworth, President, Magnolia Editions, Inc.

Donald G. Fisher, Chairman and CEO, The Gap

Donald R. Fraser, President, Inetics, Inc.

John Freeman, Ph.D., Helzel Professor of Entrepreneurship and Innovation, Haas School

Robert Frey, International Marketing Consultant

Roger Gage, Director, Cushman Realty Corp.

Charlene Geiss, Director of Finance, Drever Partners, Inc.

Richard N. Goldman, Chairman, Richard N. Goldman & Company

Alan C. Greenberg, Chairman, Bear Stearns & Co.

David Hackman, Business Consultant

Jon Hanshew, Chief Architect, SHL Systemhouse Technology Network

Lawrence B. Helzel, Member, Pacific Stock Exchange, Inc.

Stephen B. Herrick, President, SBH Associates, Inc.

Richard H. Holton, Ph.D., Professor and Dean Emeritus, Haas School

James Hornthal, President and CEO, Preview Media

Clarence W. Houghton, Adjunct Professor, Haas School

David Irons, Public Affairs Director, Haas School

Bernard Kaplan, Chairman, Marc Paul, Inc.

Melvin J. Kaplan, President, Wellington Financial Group

James A. Karr, Business Consultant

Clark Kerr, President Emeritus, University of California

David Kirshman, CPA

Jeffrey C. Lapin, President, Starwood Lodging Trust

Ori Lahav, former student, University of California

W. Howard Lester, Chairman and CEO, Williams-Sonoma, Inc.

Carl Lindner, Chairman, American Financial Corporation

Alan Lipman, President and CEO, Lipman, Carasso & Young, Inc.

James Marver, Ph.D., Senior Managing Director, Bear Stearns & Co.

Brian Maxwell, President and CEO, PowerFood, Inc.

Edward R. McCracken, Chairman and CEO, Silicon Graphics

Richard McLean, Advertising Consultant

David L. Mendel, Investment Counselor

Raymond E. Miles, Ph.D., Professor and Dean Emeritus, Haas School

Gordon Moore, President (Retired), Talbots Toyland, Inc.

Mervin G. Morris, Founder, Morris Management and Mervyn's Department Stores

Lynn V. Odland, Group Managing Partner, Deloitte & Touche

Wayne Ogata, President, Ogata Associates, Inc.

Clifford Orloff, Ph.D., President and CEO, QuickATM Corp. and Lecturer, Haas School

Ken Orton, President, Preview Media

Mark W. Perry, President and CEO, ViewStar Corporation

Matt Richtel, Business Writer, Oakland Tribune

Barry Rilliet, Vice President, Savant/Russell, Inc.

T. Gary Rogers, Chairman, Dreyer's Grand Ice Cream

Martin S. Roher, General Partner, MSR Capital Partners

Richard M. Rosenberg, Chairman and CEO, Bank of America

Gary Shapiro, Attorney at Law

Ralph J. Shapiro, Attorney at Law

William D. Sherman, Partner, Morrison & Foerster

Barclay Simpson, Chairman and CEO, Simpson Manufacturing Co., Inc.

Roger D. Snell, President and CEO, Pacific Gateway Properties, Inc.

Herbert E. Stansbury, cartoonist, Board Chairman Emeritus San Francisco Federal Savings

Elliott Steinberg, Chairman and CEO, School Properties, Inc.

Paul H. Stephens, Managing Director, Robertson Stephens & Co.

Barry S. Sternlicht, President and CEO, Starwood Capital Group

L. Jay Tenenbaum, Limited Partner, Goldman, Sachs & Co.

Chang-Lin Tien, Chancellor, University of California, Berkeley

George Turin, Sc.D., Consultant, Professor and Dean Emeritus, Engineering, UCLA and Berkeley

Richard M. Victor, Advertising Consultant

Barry L. Williams, President, Williams Pacific Ventures, Inc. and Lecturer, Haas School

Matthew L. Witte, President, Marwit Capital Corp.

Diana Zankowsky, Principal, Zankowsky & Associates

Robert J. Zembsch, Business Consultant

Harris Zimmerman, Attorney at Law

A Goal Is a Dream
with a Deadline

The Entrepreneurial Process and You

Self-assessment and an understanding of the basics of entrepreneurship are necessary before you take the leap.
Are you ready?

1.
If you hate debt,
dislike having partners,
worry about the opinions of others,
and need eight hours sleep,
forget about being an entrepreneur!

2.

Do you have confidence in the dream
and your ability to pull it off?

Can you risk all your savings,
face failure and persevere?

If the answer is yes, read on.

3.

Avoid the four deadly sins of entrepreneurship:
- not enough capital,
- not enough basic knowledge
  of the business,
- not filling a unique need,
- not enough capital.

4.

Don't fool yourself.

Entrepreneurship is not about self-employment.

It's about making money and having fun doing it.

5.

Successful entrepreneurs:
- perceive the need,
- find the market,
- invent, modify, or adapt
  the product or service,
  in that order.

6.

**Good entrepreneurs are always leaders–
sometimes good managers.**

7.

**A leader communicates the vision and
the means to attain the goal.**

A manager implements the plan.

8.

**Entrepreneurs always exude positive thinking–
even when they don't know how to meet
the next payroll.**

9.

The difference between women and men entrepreneurs
is gender.

10.

Entrepreneurship is like parenting.

If you wait until everything is right,
you'll never get started.

11.

An entrepreneurial venture is successful
only if it reaps enough profit to
expand the business manyfold.

12.

Midnight oil runs the engine of growth.

13.

Entrepreneurs actually work the hours
their attorneys bill.

14.

Think of time as money and be frugal with both.

15.

Entrepreneurs are the backbone of the future economy.

They are often treated as the tail bone,
particularly in the start-up phase.

It's the price of entry.

16.

Your concept may result from sheer genius.

But to succeed, you must organize, persevere,
… and be lucky.

17.

Luck is where preparation and opportunity meet.

18.

The driving principle of business is CFN— CASH FLOW NOW!

19.

It's a long way from a good concept to a successful company.

20.

Million dollar ideas are a dime a dozen.

The key is to find the right project *and* lead a team to implement the idea successfully.

21.

An idea without at least some element of absurdity is probably not worth further consideration.

22.

A genius is often a crackpot who hit the jackpot.

23.

Entrepreneurial genius is not finding one isolated discovery.

Real genius lies in the ability to spot the obvious–
and see the connections among several discoveries.

24.

Do what you know and do best.

Build on your specialized knowledge and experience.

25.

If you haven't identified–and thoroughly
investigated–the entrepreneurial opportunity,
don't leave your job.

26.

In most cases, the worst reason to go into business
is that you were laid off.

27.

Don't take anything from your employer, without permission, to start a new venture.

28.

Entrepreneurs don't feel they're working.

They love what they do.

Money is the score of how well they do it.

29.

It's not the destination, it's the journey.

The fun is in the doing.

30.

Seize the opportunity and begin the journey.

If you keep debating risks,
you'll never start.

31.
Just do it.

Find out later why you weren't supposed to pull it off.

32.
If at first you do succeed, try to hide your astonishment.

33.
Entrepreneurs come in all shapes, sizes, colors, ages, national origins, sexes, sexual orientations, and religions.

What counts is what's inside.

34.
Everyone loves a winner!

Planning to Implement the Dream

*After identifying and evaluating
the unique opportunity,
the entrepreneur's next step
is to plan, in detail,
how to make the business work.*

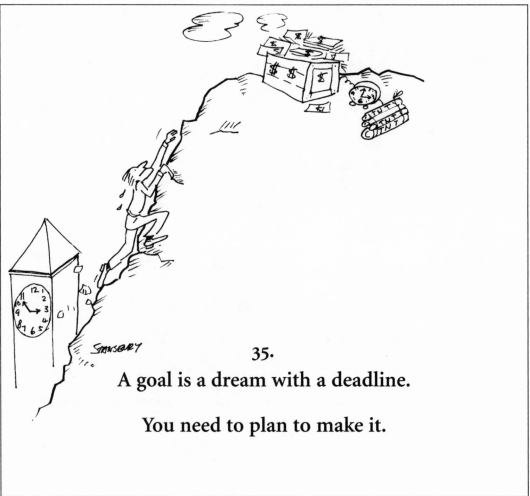

35.

A goal is a dream with a deadline.

You need to plan to make it.

36.

**Small businesses don't grow bigger
without a dreamer, planner, risk taker, and doer.**

37.

Prioritize your business goals.

**There is never enough time or money
for entrepreneurs to achieve all that
they would like to accomplish.**

38.

A business plan should answer:
- *What* is the unique product or service?
- *Where* is the market?
- *Why* will it make extraordinary profits?
- *How* much money is required from investors?
- *Who* are you and your team and
  what are your backgrounds?
- *When* will the company generate profits?

39.

The short answers to questions in #38 are
the executive summary of the business plan.

Make it convincing, correct, and concise.

The rest of the plan is supporting detail.

40.

You'll spend countless hours on a plan that
most investors toss out after reading the summary.

To capture their attention, start with the truly
unique and profitable opportunities of your company.

41.

Thorough market research will indicate whether
your product or service is unique and highly saleable.

It may confirm or shatter your plans.

42.

Investors will fund your dream only when
you can show them the potential
of the business and a large return.

43.

Credibility in a business plan is mandatory.

Avoid exaggeration and unsubstantiated statements.

Assume that the reader is more knowledgeable than you.

44.

Make your business plan a selling document
to finance your operations *and* to attract
joint ventures and key personnel.

45.

Planning can be like boot camp–you'll hate it.

**Only later in the game will you realize
it was good for you–and for the business.**

46.

Investors are impressed by your association with top-flight directors, accountants, and law firms.

Aim high. It pays.

47.

Most business plans work—on paper.

But most new businesses don't work out.

48.

Figure to spend twice as much time
and twice as much money as your plan proposes.

If the numbers still work,
you probably have a great opportunity.

49.

Never underestimate how hard it is to:

- make your company profitable, and
- once profitable, to maintain growth and profit margins.

50.

People make profits; products don't.

You bet on the jockey as well as the horse.

Plan to get top key people and reward them generously.

51.

When your plan requires a certain profit before expanding to the next milestone, make that profit before you move on.

52.

Solicit input from key employees in preparing a business plan or budget.

You can't make sound projections without the support and commitment of your team.

53.

Be conservative in estimating profits in your business plan.

But don't be too conservative, or you won't have any investors.

54.
Investors may hold you to your projections.

It's their money funding your dream.

55.
Include an exit strategy (going public or selling the business) in your business plan.

Recognize that investors, including
venture capitalists, may have a different time horizon
for cashing out than you do.

56.
Constantly measure your plan versus reality.

If they don't match, change the plan.

57.

Your pricing strategy must include the desired profit,
just as it includes the cost of sales and overhead.

58.

Provide a cushion for contingencies and
some margin for mistakes.

You'll probably need more than you plan.

59.

Reconsider the business plan or the business itself,
if financial projections cannot sustain expenditures
in employee development, R&D, and other
investments in growth.

60.

Have the courage to set high but attainable goals.

61.

Beat a plan with realistic financial goals.

Don't let an overly ambitious plan bankrupt you.

62.

Never forecast with a ruler.

Nothing in nature or business
moves in a straight line.

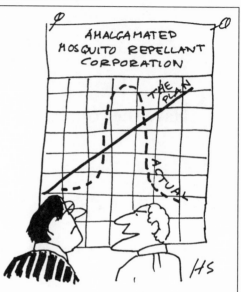

63.
In making projections, always consider
the seasonality of your business.

64.

Planning without action is a waste of time.

Action without planning can lead to disaster.

65.

Plan for an early national and international rollout.

Successful ideas, products, and services will be copied by competitors everywhere.

66.

Don't plan on overnight success.

You'll wake up to a financial nightmare.

67.

Prepare for most circumstances.

Then know you are still likely to be unprepared.

68.

Don't be a dinosaur.

Periodically redefine your business.

**Your old business plan may not fit
the changing environment.**

Raising Money

*Unless you're rich before starting
this journey, where are you going
to get the money to pull it off?
Relatives? Friends? Investors?
Venture capitalists? Your friendly
banker? Angels?
There's a business and personal price
to pay for the money,
regardless of the source.*

69.

How much of your money is invested in the venture?

It's okay if it's not much, if it's all you have.

Potential investors and lenders look for
your capital commitment.

70.

All the planning in the world can't predict
the problems and opportunities you'll face.

Get as much financing as you can the first time out.

Money may not be available when you need it
for the second round.

71.

You may have to pay an extraordinarily high price
for loans and capital in a startup.

Not all money is created equal.

72.

An entrepreneur always needs money,
either for growth or survival.

73.

Avoid friends and family, if possible, as investors.

It's a "lose-lose" proposition.

If you succeed, they probably won't thank you.
If you fail, they may shun you.

74.

Infusion of capital and talent makes
small businesses bigger.

To get both requires giving up some ownership.

A smaller interest in a substantial company beats
100 percent of little or nothing.

75.

Encourage your large investors to join your
board of directors.

Most investors are experienced business people.

Once they've invested in you, they are willing
to help you solve problems.

76.

Venture capital companies are more likely to invest
in businesses that are poised for take-off.

It's difficult to obtain seed money
unless you have a great track record
in a high-growth industry.

77.

Don't accept investors just because they have money.

Check their reputation. You may have to live with them
through difficult times.

78.

Accepting an investor's check just marks
the beginning of the relationship.

Regular communications, in good times and bad,
are essential to maintaining this delicate partnership.

79.

Your best investment is in the equity of your company.

Where else do you have so much control and
knowledge of an investment?

80.

Retain as much equity in your company as possible,
particularly in the early stages.

If you sell equity early,
you will rarely get it back at your original cost.

81.

Most entrepreneurs are faced with the dilemma of:

- selling equity,
- borrowing money with a personal guaranty, or
- hocking the house, the spouse, or the kids.

82.

Consider raising money through a sale-leaseback of some assets that are not hypothecated (hocked).

It's expensive. Use this and other fancy financing plans only when your banker turns you down.

Watch the fine print.

83.

Avoid complicated financial arrangements.

They make it difficult to attract loans and capital in the future.

84.

In borrowing money from a bank and extending credit
to customers, remember credit's four Cs:

Character, Capacity, Capital, and Collateral.

85.

When you go for a loan,
plan on answering these four questions:
- How much money will you need?
- How will you use it?
- How will you repay it?
- When will you repay it?

86.

Try to avoid personal guaranties on company debt.

Good luck!

87.

Develop as many financing options and contingency plans as possible.

If one option collapses, another may support the business through tough times.

88.

Cultivate your bank loan officer. Make her an auxiliary member of your management team.

Keep her informed about your business, including all internally prepared financial statements.

STANSBURY

Management
Maxims

The skills required to operate a business successfully are often different from those required to launch the venture. Not knowing what you don't know may be a blessing in a startup, but a disaster as the company grows. Good entrepreneurs recognize this and follow these battle-tested management rules.

89.

Business excellence begins with
how high you set your standards.

90.

Anticipate major waves of change and
position your business to ride them.

91.

Never delegate:
- creating the vision,
- selecting the team,
- monitoring, motivating,
  and rewarding, and
- being the boss.

92.

When you delegate, don't dump.

Give authority, responsibility, budget, and deadline.

Monitor progress.

93.

Don't manage outcomes;
manage the processes to get there.

94.

The status quo is the strongest force in life–
and in business.

Work with or around it.

95.

Hire a manager as soon as possible
to deal with day-to-day operations.

Your responsibility is to lead and
plan for tomorrow's opportunities.

96.

Make necessary changes early in a project.

Delaying change can cost time and money.

97.

Change and pain are often synonymous.

Success demands you deal with both.

98.

Change usually requires creative destruction.

Managing change demands self-management.

It's tough on everyone, including you.

99.

Every crisis creates challenges *and* opportunities.

Meet the challenges.

Take advantage of the opportunities.

100.

Ask the tough business and personal question
even if it's sensitive.

The longer you wait, the tougher it gets.

101.

Don't upset the processes that are right
in your haste to fix the things that are wrong.

102.

**Never use a ten-dollar bill as a torch
to find nickels in the snow.**

103.

Take genuine joy in the success of those
who work with and for you.

104.

When in doubt, say "no."

It's much easier to change later.

105.

In times of disaster, be candid.

In times of triumph, be modest.

106.

Be wise enough to value other people's ideas.

Then be strong enough to give them credit.

107.

Accept blame for failures,
your own and those of your employees and partners.

Or else don't accept any of the rewards
that go with success.

108.

Stay humble. "Thou will do well in business as long as Thou dost not believe thine own odor is perfume."

109.

Employ trickle-down ethics.

The more there is at the top,
the more there will be throughout.

110.

Get out of the ivory tower.

The air is thin up there,
and the view is far too remote.

111.

A strong leader can steer a company
in the wrong direction.

But *only* a strong leader can steer a company
in any direction.

112.

Nothing breeds success like success itself.

Keep rolling the dice.

113.

Press your winners, nix your losers.

114.

You don't always have to make a commitment;
but once you do, keep it!

115.

Act on mistakes as soon as you recognize them.

Nothing aggravates errors like time.

116.

Accentuate the positive; eliminate the negative.

117.

Think of suppliers as partners.

118.

Stick to your expertise and experience whenever you consider new products, large purchases, and mergers or acquisitions.

119.

Understand every feature of a product or service that you want to buy before you compare prices.

120.

Possession is 98 percent of the law.

Don't pay for work before it's completed and delivered.

121.

Before telling a "secret," remember that
others treat "secrets" just like you do.

122.

Confide secrets only when you want them leaked.

123.

If you want a successful personal relationship,
look to a friend, spouse, or relative.

If you want a successful business relationship,
look somewhere else.

124.

Don't be fooled by success
when you have the market all to yourself.

The test is how you and your organization perform
when the market is competitive.

125.

Don't assume tomorrow will turn out like today.

If you do, you're living in the past.

126.

You can't forecast turns in the road ahead
by concentrating on the rear-view mirror.

127.

Resolve disputes early.

Avoid litigation whenever possible.

128.

Litigation is always costly and time-consuming,
and rarely profitable or productive.

129.

Cut expenses all the time,
even when business is great.

130.

Don't let the big guys outspend you on things
that money can't buy.

A smile, a firm handshake, integrity, enthusiasm—
the other intangibles count, too.

131.

In publicly announcing a major change
in your business, be sure to inform employees,
suppliers, and customers simultaneously.

They have more at stake than the general public.

132.

Entrepreneurs can't stop thinking about business.

Not all ideas and solutions to problems
are born at the office.

133.

Keep a memo pad or recorder handy in your car, shower, night stand, or pocket.

134.

Keep detailed notes of meetings and telephone calls and file them carefully.

Your memory is not that good that you can recall conversations of months and years gone by.

135.

Don't say you can't do it.

Find out how you can do it, and then decide whether it's worth the cost.

136.

Unnecessary and unaccounted for expenditures
are unacceptable.

Everyone, especially you, must understand why
and where they spend the firm's money.

Your behavior sets the standard for your people.

137.

Beware of your own complacency.

138.

Greed can be the executioner of success.

Your customers, suppliers, and employees
will be at the guillotine.

139.

Balance your perspective with interests
outside the business, particularly community interests.

Make the time.

You can spare a couple of hours
out of your eighty-hour work week.

140.

No good deeds shall go unpunished.

But you must do them anyway.

Decisions!
Decisions!

*Once you've decided to take the risk
of starting the venture, all the incidental
"CYA" politics of decision making
become irrelevant. Quick decisions and
negotiations, essential to the growth and
survival of the business, are the norm.
Lengthy deliberations become the exception.
There's no time or need to look back.
You'd be scared to death if you did.*

141.

In making major decisions,
balance the needs of the "big three"–
customers, employees, and investors.

142.
Professionals can help with major decisions.

Get more than one opinion before you decide.

143.
On major issues, it's always best to make a good decision.

A bad decision may be better
than no decision.

144.

Choosing to take no action must be viewed
as a conscious decision.

145.

Procrastination on major decisions can be costly.

Hasty, ill-conceived actions can be more costly.

146.

Learn which problems and opportunities demand
prompt action and which merit procrastination.

147.

Delay some business decisions as long as is prudent.

Often a problem will solve itself.

148.

Don't make a decision in anger.

Act after a good night's sleep.

149.

Think twice. Act once.

150.

Ninety-two percent of what you worry about won't happen.

151.

Negotiations mostly entail
who, when, where, how, and how much.

Decisions require a yes or a no.

152.

Not all decisions require negotiation.

All negotiations require decisions.

153.

Always negotiate on a deadline.

Concessions on both sides of the table will usually be made when time is running out.

154.

Look to the big issues and big bucks in a deal.

Don't sweat the small stuff.

155.

In any negotiation, always leave something on the table, as well as your counterpart's pride.

156.

If you reach the third negotiating session and you're not close to agreement on most issues, odds are that you can't close the deal.

157.

Dealing is feeling; logic alone rarely makes a good deal.

158.

If you talk too much, let your partner
(or your attorney) do the negotiating.

159.

Don't agree to a contract that is unethical or unfair,
even though it may be legal. It's bad business.

160.

Keep to both the letter and the spirit of your agreements.

161.

When you enter a deal, be aware of the costs and complications should it fail.

It's always easier to start
a relationship than to end one.

People, Pay, and Perks

People are always the entrepreneur's most important asset. Finding and keeping the best can mean the difference between success and failure.

162.
To start, it's money and people–in that order.

To last, it's people and money.

163.
It is better to have a grade B product
with grade A management than vice versa.

164.
Hire smart. It's a lot easier than managing tough.

165.

Hire people who have little regard for the status quo and who are not afraid of innovating.

166.

Employ people who care–a lot.

Look for ambition, intelligence, and self-motivation.

167.

Hire slowly and carefully.

Then you won't have to fire quickly.

168.

Hire proven talent whenever available–
even if you have to stretch to get them.

169.

For short-term tasks, hire temporary help or
experienced professionals who "moonlight."

170.

Be wary of perennial job switchers.

171.

Venture capitalists are not just a source of money.
They know talented people.

Ask their help in finding the right people
to build a top management team.

172.

Don't rely on the first interview.
It may only tell you if you like the person.

The second or third may tell you
whether you can work together.

173.

You'll learn 70 percent of
what you need to know about a person
in the first 10 percent of the relationship.

174.

Surround yourself with people who complement
your strengths and shore up your weaknesses.

175.

Choose the right partners.
You're married to them–for better or for worse.

176.

Hire people with the ability to replace you.

177.

Don't hire only MBAS**–also hire** PSDS
(people who are Poor, Smart,
and have a Desire to be rich).

178.

Hire people who have imagination for key positions,
even though they may not have an MBA
or an advanced degree.

179.

A business school cannot teach
common sense, creativity, or imagination.

These are uncommon talents.

180.

MBAS, however, *can* have all the right instincts,
drive, desire, and determination,
in addition to their education.

181.

Things get done because someone with conviction
uses more effort.

182.

Make certain that employees understand one key
financial equation: profitability equals job security.

183.

Share financial goals and results monthly
with employees.

Compare projected sales, profits, and cash flow
against actual performance,
department by department.

184.

Energize, excite, and coach rather than
enervate, depress, and control.

185.

Make employees know they are the company.

If they don't work well, it won't either.

186.

Allow employees to try and fail.

Your success relies on their entrepreneurship.

187.
Have an open door policy.

Great insight can come from employees
who walk into your office to tell you
of opportunities and problems.

188.
Be friendly with your employees, but not familiar.

Remember the adage:
"Good fences make good neighbors."

189.
Hire managers whose personalities you want to see
reflected in the business.

190.

An organization chart only shows the way
the players line up before the ball is snapped.

191.

Empower employees to make decisions
within their responsibilities.

Measure and reward their results, not their activity.

192.

Power is a constantly shifting commodity
in any organization.

So is loyalty.

193.

Power and authority in a company are up for grabs.

Worst is that *nobody* takes them,
better is that *you* take them,
best is that *everyone* takes them.

194.

Tie compensation to performance.

When employees exceed stated expectations,
reward them.

When they don't meet minimum expectations,
terminate them.

195.

Ingenuity, innovation, and success in risk taking
merit special consideration.

196.

Reward people for meaningful accomplishments
with cash or stock options.

Certificates of appreciation are nice,
but they don't pay the mortgage.

197.
Never underestimate how difficult it is to
keep your best employees.

It requires TLC (tender loving care),
recognition, communication, loyalty, and money.

Not necessarily in that order.

198.
Use equity as an incentive to ensure that your employees
become entrepreneurs within the firm.

Reserve a generous amount of shares at the outset for
key management additions.

199.
Don't vest employees 100 percent
during the first few years of their employment
in your stock option, profit-sharing, and pension plans.

That way, you separate loyal employees
from the job jumpers.

200.
Don't hire anyone you can't fire.

201.

Think twice before you hire your children or close relatives.

If you do hire them, they should be treated just like any other employee.

Good luck!

202.

Get people to match your principles, not the reverse.

203.

Make all communications clear, concise,
and easy to understand.

204.

Convene a meeting only when you need
a group to accomplish the task.

Substitute electronic mail for
routine informational meetings.

205.

Encourage competition within your teams.

The contest often unleashes creative forces.

206.

Negotiate peace between two warring associates;
or one or both will have to go.

207.

If you decide someone must be fired,
don't procrastinate.

208.

Anticipate that people, with ingrained behavior, will act as they acted before.

Leopards do not change their spots.

Bad traits often remain or get worse.

209.

Don't tolerate morale-destroying gossip, unauthorized release of confidential information, and rumor-mongering in your organization.

This is not a free speech issue. Loose lips sink ships.

210.

Don't abandon employees with great work skills just because of poor people skills.

Put them in an environment that emphasizes the work, not the interaction.

211.

Perform personnel exit interviews.

They'll tell you what you hate to hear
but need to know.

212.

Educate your people to understand
and anticipate the future.

Never before in history has change been coming so fast.

213.

Build a work force with an absolutely infinite capacity to improve everything.

Sell! Sell! Sell!

Nothing really happens in a business
until the customer says "Yes."
Some tips on making the sale.

214.

The best way to grow your business is with your customers' money.

215.

Fully appreciate your sales and marketing staff.

Profits can't start until a sale is made.

216.

Selling is making the sale happen.

Marketing is getting the customer ready to accept the product and the sales person.

217.

Sell with sincerity.

218.

Know your customer's needs.

Sell benefits or solutions, not products or features.

Your advertising should emphasize these points.

219.

You have only one opportunity to
make a good first impression.

220.

Most great sales people are problem solvers.

They are PSers, not BSers.

221.

In hiring marketing and sales people, differentiate the problem solvers from the pitch men.

222.

As a sales person, ask a lot of questions.

One of the best is: "How can I help you?"

223.

Replace the phrase, "I don't know," with,
"Let me check and find out."

224.

Tell customers how good you are,
not how bad your competition is.

There is no long-term advantage in knocking someone.

225.

Good ethics are good business.

Treat everyone fairly, every time, all the time.

226.

Many people buy on emotion.

Let your sales presentation
offer rationale and reassurance.

227.

Nothing substitutes for the benefits of personal contact.

The phone is for phone calls; your face is for sales calls.

228.

Turn a cold call into a warm call.

229.

If sales prospects have a lot of time to "schmooze," they are probably not serious about buying.

230.

Don't take a sales call rejection personally.

You don't know if they are rejecting you
or the product, or if your timing is bad.

So give yourself the benefit of the doubt.

231.

Consider a "no" as an opportunity
to find another solution
to the customer's problem.

A "know" counters a "no."

232.

Sales people should be product detectives.

The customers will offer ideas for your next product.

233.

Be in the business of selling the high-priced *or*
the low-priced product.

There is little room for a business in between.

234.

You don't have to be first in a market to be a winner.

Take advantage of better products and service,
as well as the mistakes of your competition,
to capture your share of the market.

235.

Marketing is planning and executing:

- concepts,
- products,
- pricing,
- promotion,
- advertising,
- distribution, and
- sales programs.

236.

Require your marketing people to get out
of the office and make sales calls.

They'll learn a lot about the customers,
the competition, and your sales force.

237.

Beware of too much market intuition.

Test, measure, and quantify every
assumption, claim, and expectation.

Then, trust your gut.

238.

Market research seeks the answer to:
- Who will buy the product?
- What are the customers' needs?
- Why buy this product over competitors'?
- How much will the customers pay?
- Where will they go to buy?

239.

Market research isn't rocket science.

You are only looking for answers to
how customers react to your product.

240.

Many entrepreneurs belatedly use market research
when their new products aren't selling.

241.

Marketing consumer products
requires substantial budgets for continuing
advertising and promotion programs.

Don't enter this game without plenty of
cash or an alliance with the big guys.

242.

Don't be afraid of alliances with
dominant marketers in your field.

Even with the best new consumer product in the world,
no one will beat a path to your door—unless you have
marketing and distribution power.

243.

Entrepreneurs use channel marketing—
packaging the same product in various ways
through different kinds of distribution—
to increase sales, profits, and customer feedback.

Sounds simple? It ain't.

244.

In direct marketing, the manufacturer or distributor
becomes the retailer and sells the customer
through television, computer, mail order, telephone,
and company-owned stores.

Sometimes they are super discounters.

245.

Who pays retail list prices today?

Is it any wonder so many retail startups fail?

246.

Direct mail, using current and targeted lists, can be a most scientific and predictable form of selling.

Catalog sales are a prime example.

You need lots of chips and expertise to play this game.

247.
Never forget that advertising is a
category of marketing—never an end in itself.

248.
If your business isn't worth advertising,
advertise it for sale.

249.

The four most powerful words in advertising are:

- you,
- new,
- revolutionary, and
- free.

250.

Keep hammering with the same successful ad,
even if it bores you.

Many of your target customers may be just
beginning to recognize your product and you.

251.

There is no greater credibility bridge than
a money-back guarantee.

252.

In markets that you cannot penetrate with
your own distribution system, find joint venturers,
franchisees, distributors, and licensees.

253.

Never count your customers' money
when setting pricing policies.

254.

You know your product is properly priced
when you can sell all you can make or buy–
and still make your profit goals.

255.

If you think that every sales call you make is successful,
you're probably not making enough calls.

256.

Figure that it takes three calls to close a sale.

257.

Learn to make sales by closing early and often.

258.

Listening is often more important than talking.

259.

Once you've closed the sale, shut up.

We no longer have a sales problem . . .
We ran out of customers.

Keeping Customers Happy

The entrepreneur's goal is to make
customers feel they are indispensable.
There is no business without them.
Some tricks of the trade follow.

260.

Treat the customer like an invited guest in your home.

261.

Retain old customers.

It is many times less expensive
than adding new ones.

262.

Be known as *customer-driven.*

Put the customers first and
design the business around their satisfaction.

Word-of-mouth referral is your best advertising.

263.

Expand and diversify your customer base.

You are vulnerable if you depend on a single market
or a few large customers.

264.

It is safer to have fifty small-volume customers than two
or three large accounts for the same total amount of sales.

You'll lose accounts for reasons beyond your control.

265.

Bend over backwards to help customers,
but don't let their demands break you.

266.

Fill the customer's order:

- correctly
- on time
- the first time.

267.

Deliver what you promise.

Don't deliver something less, something different, something smaller, or something larger.

268.

The customer is always right,
but watch your pockets!

269.

The customer's job is to whine;
your job is to make it a happy tune.

270.

Customers take their cue from employees.

Keeping morale high raises loyalty and sales.

271.

Grow your customer base and then your overhead;
not the other way around.

272.
Sell added security to customers.

They may never use 24-hour service, but they will buy more readily if it's available.

273.
Listen when customers complain.

Otherwise they're likely to find an ear with your competition.

274.
Establish a "no hassles" return policy.

Fix it, exchange it, or return the money.

Make unhappy customers happy
and they'll be yours forever.

Developing and Perfecting the Product

Keeping the entrepreneur's product line or service ahead of the competition's–again, again, and again–requires talent in product planning, research and development, engineering, and manufacturing–plus some calculated risk taking. Las Vegas is easy compared to this game. Want to try your luck?

275.
Innovate and differentiate.

Bet on your vision for the future.

Imitate only as a last resort.

276.
Coordinate design, engineering, manufacturing,
and marketing *at the beginning*
of new product development.

It saves time and money every time.

277.

Dazzling engineering or design cannot guarantee
a successful product.

Test whether the customers and the trade will buy
the product in sufficient quantities and
at a price that provides ample profit margins.

278.

Build quality through excellent engineering
and manufacturing.

Inspection, while essential, cannot cure faulty engineering.

279.

Quality is excellence; and excellence of
your product or service is essential for survival.

280.

In creating a product, you usually have
only one or two sides of this triangle:
speed, economy, and excellence.

Rarely all three.

281.

If you provide better quality, service, and delivery,
your business will expand beyond your expectations.
If you don't, a competitor will.

282.

To improve manufacturing quality,
cross-train workers in several skills.

They can solve problems together,
and substitute for each other when necessary.

283.

Know how to fix the products that are returned.
Incorporate this knowledge into redesign and
manufacturing to solve the problem.

284.

Build a product to last for a long
but not eternal commercial life.

Lifetime guarantees are not economically practical.

285.

Risk showing your fledgling product to
established companies in your industry.

You have much more to learn from them
than they do from you.

286.

Whether it's broke or not, fix it.
Make it better to beat competition.

287.

Create and market the first product that
makes your current product line obsolete.

If you don't, someone else will.

288.

Good research and engineering can spot the obvious
and sometimes use it in ways no one else has.

289.

Product improvement need not be radical to have radical significance.

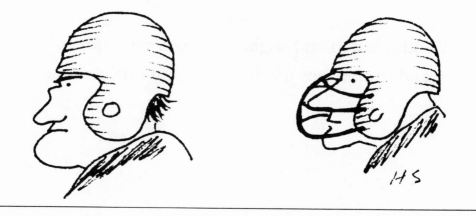

290.

Anything old can be new again,
when you add marketable features.

291.

To fit today's fast-paced, high-tech world,
change your definition of long-term product planning.

Two years is about right, three years is a bit long,
and five years may be eternity.

292.

It is better to have no research than bad research.

Then you can trust your gut to find better solutions.

293.
Don't put all your R&D eggs in one basket.

Spread risk by buying research or
licensing new inventions from others.

294.
A common barrier to implementing any great idea
is NIH (Not Invented Here).

Purchasing solutions may be more cost-effective
than inventing them.

295.

Do what you and your people do best;
use suppliers to do the rest.

You don't need your own operation
for every part of the business.

296.

Protect proprietary R&D, trade secrets, customer lists
with reasonable agreements with employees.

297.

Don't license your proven technology to unreliable firms.

Inferior manufacturing, price cutting, and poor service
will damage you and the industry.

298.

Evaluate all the risks, rewards, and investments
before you pioneer new products.

There are few wealthy pioneers, many poor ones,
and only a handful in between.

299.

Doubling money in five years
is a good return for an investor.

A hundred-fold return, or even more,
on investment sounds right for a revolutionary product
that creates a large new market.

That's why some successful people bet on high-risk,
high-return research and development.

Going Global

The United States, with the world's largest GNP, has about 20 percent of global output. The entrepreneur, with a unique product line that has international appeal, would be foolish to ignore the rest of the world. This applies to any entrepreneur, anywhere.

300.
Compete globally.

Your customers and suppliers, no matter how distant,
can be as close as the nearest phone.

301.
When doing business abroad,
you are a guest of the host country.

Never forget it!

302.
Never assume that business
is conducted in a foreign country
just as it is at home.

303.

Learn about your host's people by reading
about their history and culture.

You will be more sensitive to their customs and feelings.

304.

Always assume that time will be handled
differently in a foreign country

305.

Never hurry a customer
so that you can catch your flight home.

306.

Always compliment a national's English;
correct it only on request.

307.

Fluency in English does not automatically
qualify a host national for a job.

308.

Foreign language fluency doesn't qualify employees
for a job abroad that
they could not fill at home.

309.

Prior to your first trip to a foreign country,
learn twenty to fifty key words and numbers.

Start with "please" and "thank you."

310.

Never criticize a host country's politics, sexual mores–
or anything else.

311.

Observe how nationals greet one another and do likewise,
even if it feels awkward.

312.

Latin Americans may refuse to do business with you
if you are too serious.

So lighten up and slow down.

313.

In Asia, learn when "maybe" really means "no."

314.

You can't listen enough.

Be sensitive to what your hosts are *really* saying.

315.

A good sense of humor travels well.

But some jokes don't.

316.

Use visual aids in presentations abroad.

One picture is worth a thousand words
that you probably don't know.

317.

Keep away from consultants who tell you they have
special connections in the highest levels of government.

318.

Try to speak the local language even if you do so poorly.

It tells people you know how difficult
it is for them to speak English.

319.

The national employees will often claim that
only nationals can be effective in their own country.

Don't buy this.

320.

When opening an office abroad,
bring your own accountant, but hire a local attorney.

321.

Some managing directors abroad feel that
they are operating their own business,
but using your capital and know-how.

This can be good for the company, but protect yourself.

322.

Be especially careful when selecting
foreign joint venture partners.

This is an opportunity for an expensive mistake
that can be difficult to rectify.

323.

Staff your new foreign office with
seasoned international and national professionals.

Avoid people who may see the position
as a paid vacation abroad.

324.

Plow some of your foreign profits
back into host countries for continued growth.

It's good business and terrific public relations.

Tough Times

Most successful entrepreneurs go through several setbacks and sometimes failures before hitting pay dirt. All entrepreneurs experience recessions. Here are some guidelines for getting through tough times.

325.

Never, never, never quit, no matter how tough it gets,
as long as the business has a chance to succeed.

326.

An entrepreneur rarely succeeds
without first going through
disappointment or failures.

The best recover fastest.

327.

When you're in a hole, don't dig.

328.

Face disasters early.

Tell the truth.

Bite the bullet.

329.

Character and integrity are the cornerstones
of business trust.

They shine through–particularly during tough times.

330.

Make it easy for your people to tell you bad news.

The sooner you know, the sooner you can act.

331.

You can learn more about people
in two months of bad times
than in five years of good times.

332.

In tough times, trim judiciously and maintain expenses
that keep the business running.

333.

Don't cut expenses across the board.

Customer service should never be curtailed.

334.

Don't reach for an off-the-shelf cure
before you know how serious the problem is.

335.

You can't pay bills with delinquent receivables
and slow moving inventory.

336.

Earnings, without positive cash flow,
can be an illusion.

337.
If you have to choose between liquidity–
the ability to pay bills–
and profitability, choose liquidity.

It will provide survival.

338.

Avoid the downsizing double whammy:
your best people desert;
less competent ones dig in.

339.

When asking to extend a loan, promise your bankers
a payment schedule that you can make or exceed.

Your credibility and future relationship are on the line.

340.

If you get caught in a trap, get out.

Don't try to take the cheese with you.

341.

Beware of the "give it time–it's too early to tell"
syndrome. Odds are, something is wrong.

Find it and fix it, or pull the plug.

342.

Don't wait for bankruptcy to face and
admit financial problems.

Seek cooperation *early* from creditors, investors,
and employees.

343.

If you can't pay your bills and can't get new funds, seek time and breathing space by reorganizing under Chapter 11 of the bankruptcy laws.

Many companies succeed after reorganization.

Conserving Cash and Keeping Score

Tight controls and accurate number crunching are essential for the entrepreneur's survival in a competitive world. The game is cash flow and profits. Some advice on how to win.

344.
Cash is cash. Everything else is a journal entry.

345.
Conserve cash by leasing equipment, autos,
and other fixed assets,
or by buying used equipment at bargain prices.

346.
Stock minimum inventory for new products.

Minimize your cash exposure.

347.

Know your numbers cold and
base your decisions on the details.

348.

Do your "due diligence" on any transaction
you have to evaluate.

Remember: "In the land of the blind,
the one-eyed man is king."

349.

If you don't understand something fully,
don't buy it, sell it, trade it,
or express an opinion about it.

350.

Don't just learn to read financial statements–
know how to analyze them.

351.

Success is never having to apologize
for your gross margins.

352.

High gross profit margins offer lots of room
to make mistakes and still make a profit.

353.
Beware of sales growth without
corresponding net income growth.
This is your wake-up call for
major management moves.

354.
Get sales projections on new products
from your optimistic sales and marketing people.

Discount their projections before buying inventory.

If you are wrong and sales are brisk,
you can apologize all the way to the bank.

355.

Be conservative with your profit and loss statements.

Never report income before you earn it.

Always write off expenses when you incur them.

356.

Write off your research and development
costs as you incur them.

Your banker does not view them as an asset.

357.

Find a secondary market for your obsolete
and slow-moving inventory and sell into it–
even if you don't recoup your costs.

358.

Be aggressive but polite with "slow-pay" customers.

The squeaky wheel really gets the grease.

359.

Telephone calls to delinquent accounts are
far more effective than letters.

You get information from a call.

360.

Savings on expenses generally go to
the bottom line as profits.

When you're a public company, they are magnified
by the price-earnings multiple the stock carries.

361.

Manage your liabilities as efficiently
as you manage your assets.

362.

Take all cash discounts offered–
but pay on the last possible day.

363.

A larger-than-anticipated loss may mean
it's time to close an operation.

Don't throw good money after bad.

364.

Have all your employees learn to use technology
to gather information and make decisions faster,
with more accuracy and less cost.

365.

Beware the *x*'s of specialized software.
It is usually e*x*otic, typically e*x*pensive,
and often e*x*cessive.

366.

Expedite your deliveries and invoicing.

Delays cost money.

367.

Insist on receiving your financial data within
fifteen days after the end of each month.

You need to act on the information
to keep your business competitive and profitable.

368.

If you're not diligent, your financial statement
can be a fiscal snapshot taken through a distorted lens
and then retouched.

369.

Retain an experienced insurance broker
who understands your business
or takes the time to learn it.

370.

Premiums vary among insurers for the same coverage.

It pays to shop.

371.

Insure all employees having a fiduciary responsibility with a fidelity bond.

Dishonest employees have broken many companies.

Don't assume it can't happen to you.

372.

Cellular phones are radio-based and
do not have the privacy of wired telephones.

Never broadcast company financial data,
your credit card number, or other
confidential information over a cellular phone.

373.

Seek a chief finanical officer
with a split personality–
to charm the money people *and*
be as tough as nails on costs and expenses.

374.
Retain four talented professionals you trust:
an attorney, a banker, a tax-savvy CPA,
and an insurance broker.

Sometimes a psychiatrist.

375.
God is in the details.

The Harvest or the Bail-Out

Entrepreneurs should plan to exit with a pot of gold. Several options are outlined for a profitable harvest. Sometimes fate is unkind and the pot is empty. A little philosophy follows for the entrepreneur who doesn't make it—this time.

376.

The entrepreneur's goal is to create
a successful business *and* a significant
realizable value for the company.

377.

Just as there are windows of opportunity
to start a company,
there are also windows to cash out.

378.

Make certain that working partners
and investors in your company
share your vision for the exit strategy.

379.

One of the most important assets of a business–
not on the balance sheet–
can be its active customer list.

Remember this at harvest time.

380.

Timing is everything.

Perceptions and investment fads may create an
unrealistically high value for the company.

Take the money and run.

381.

The time to start worrying
is when things are going well.

382.

When you *know* it's time to sell out,
it's probably too late to get the best deal.

383.

Go public with your company
if you wish to provide liquidity and valuation
for the investors, employees, and yourself.

384.

You can raise needed capital for the company
on favorable terms in a good public market.

385.

Forget about going public if you covet your privacy,
dislike pressure to maintain growth quarterly
and annually, and are sensitive about
answering questions from stockholders and analysts.

386.

Rethink your options if you want to maintain
ownership control and slower paced growth.

387.

If you go public, go truly public.
Float enough stock to
create a good market for your shareholders.

388.

Use public relations to keep your name
and reputation golden, particularly before and after
becoming a publicly-owned company.

389.

Merging with a large publicly-held company
gives the investors and the entrepreneur:

- liquidity,
- usually a tax-free exchange, and
- sometimes a good long-term investment.

390.

Selling out for cash offers:
- the highest liquidity,
- payment of income taxes, and
- problems of investment of
the net proceeds of sale.

391.

Selling out to key people,
through a leveraged management buyout (LBO),
may provide both investors
and the entrepreneur with a good harvest.

However, an LBO usually loads the company with debt.
This can lead to downsizing and other problems.

392.

Selling the company to employees via a leveraged
employee stock ownership plan (ESOP) can
present some of the same problems as the LBO.

393.

Keeping the business in the family is great
if your working partners and investors agree
that your offspring are superstars.

394.

Pick the most competent people to run the business if the family wants to maintain control of the company.

395.

The decision on succession to the CEO of a family-owned business should be guided by someone who is neither family nor working for the company.

396.

Success is never final; failure is rarely fatal.

397.
Tomorrow is another day.

Wrap it up and close the doors when you determine
that the venture cannot make it.

398.
You often recover from a loss of money,
but rarely from a loss of integrity.

399.
When the bottom falls out, pick yourself up,
dust yourself off, and start all over again.

400.

Win or lose, the experience of being
an entrepreneur is unforgettable.

Try it!

401.

What have we but our dreams?

Glossary

after-tax cash flow   The expected net return from an investment project.

asset-based financing   Financing secured by long-term assets.

average rate of return   A comparison of the average net income of a company to average investment.

bankruptcy code   A federal law (11 U.S.C.A.) for the benefit and relief of creditors and their debtors in which the latter are unable or unwilling to pay their debts.

book value   The original cost of an asset less its accumulated depreciation. Book value of net worth represents book value of assets less liabilities.

cash flow   Cash receipts less disbursements.

common stock   A class of corporate stock that represents the residual ownership of the corporation.

corporation   A legal entity created by or under the authority of the laws of a state. The corporation is distinct from the persons who comprise it (shareholders).

cost of capital   The minimum rate of return that a company must earn on its assets to satisfy investors. Also may refer to the cost of raising money.

current assets   Property, including cash, that will be or could be converted into cash, in the normal operation of the business, or earlier, usually within one year, e.g., cash, accounts receivable, inventory.

current liabilities   An obligation that will be paid in the ordinary course of business or within one year.

current ratio   A measure of the liquidity of a company found by dividing current assets by current liabilities.

Many of these definitions come from the glossary of *Entrepreneurship*, by Hisrich and Peters, 2nd Edition, 1992, Irwin, and are used with permission of Robert D. Hisrich, Ph.D.

c.y.a.   Cover your backside.

debt-to-equity ratio   The proportion of debt to equity in a firm's financial structure.

earnings per share   A measure of profitability derived by dividing the net income of the company by the average number of shares outstanding.

employee stock ownership plan (ESOP)   A type of employees' qualified profit sharing plan that invests in the securities of the employer.

equity   The portion of the balance sheet representing ownership that includes capital stock, preferred stock, retained earnings, and certain other reserve or surplus accounts.

factoring   Sale of accounts receivable to a bank or finance company.

financial leverage   The relationship between borrowed funds and shareholder's equity. (When there is a high proportion of debt-to-equity in a company, it is highly leveraged, which increases the financial risk of the firm.)

financial risk   The risk that a firm may not be able to meet its financial obligations.

going concern   A company whose operation is expected to continue.

golden parachute   A provision to protect existing officers and directors of a company from removal in the event of a takeover. Often a large sum of money is involved upon removal.

gross profit margin   The difference between net sales and the cost of goods sold, expressed as a percentage of net sales.

inventory turnover ratio   A ratio measuring the number of times the inventory of a company is turned (sold each year).

investment value   The theoretic intrinsic value of an asset or company.

insolvency   The inability or lack of means to pay debts as they become due.

joint venture   An agreement between companies to enter into a partnership for a specific project.

leveraged buyout (LBO)   A buyout in which the purchaser borrows funds to buy the stock of a company and then uses the resources of the company to repay the loan.

liquidity   The ability of a company to meet its current financial obligations.

market value   The price investors are willing to pay for the securities of a company.

merger   A combination of two or more companies in which one company survives, retaining its identity.

net present value   The present value of expected cash flows discounted at the cost of capital less the investment outlay.

net profit margin   The percentage of profit earned for each dollar of sales calculated by dividing net income by net sales.

partnership   A business owned by two or more persons that is not a corporation.

payback period   The number of years required to return an investment outlay.

preferred stock   Stock representing one class of ownership on a company; generally has fixed dividends and/or liquidation rights over the common shares.

present value   The current value of dollars that will be received in the future.

price/earnings (P/E) ratio   A ratio determined by dividing the market price of a stock by its earnings. A high price/earnings ratio of a company indicates that investors expected good company growth.

pro forma financial statements   Projected financial statements of future periods of the operations of the company.

reorganization (Chapter 11)   When a debtor business entity realizes that it will become insolvent or will be unable to pay its debts as they mature, it can petition for reorganization under Chapter 11 of the Bankruptcy Code.

return on assets   The net income divided by the assets of a company.

return on equity   The net income divided by the equity of a company.

seed money   An initial contribution toward the financing or capital requirements of a new business.

sole proprietorship   An unincorporated business owned by one person.

term loan   A loan from a commercial bank with a usual maturity of five years or less commonly used for plant and equipment, working capital, or debt repayment.

time value of money   The principle that money received in the present is worth more than the same amount received in the future.

variable cost   Cost that changes in direct proportion to the number of units made.

vested   Fixed, complete, not contingent.

venture capital   Funding for new companies, or others embarking on new or turnaround ventures, that entail investment risk but offer the potential for high future returns.

working capital   The dollar amount of a company's current assets less current liabilities.